50 Mindful Eating Bowls for Home

By: Kelly Johnson

- Quinoa & Roasted Veggie Bowl
- Buddha Bowl with Hummus
- Mediterranean Chickpea Bowl
- Green Goddess Grain Bowl
- Spicy Thai Peanut Bowl
- Protein-Packed Lentil Bowl
- Miso Tofu & Brown Rice Bowl
- Roasted Sweet Potato & Kale Bowl
- Avocado & Black Bean Bowl
- Cauliflower Rice & Turmeric Bowl
- Hearty Farro & Mushroom Bowl
- Vegan Poke Bowl with Edamame
- Spiced Chickpea & Spinach Bowl
- Greek-Inspired Orzo Bowl
- Rainbow Nourish Bowl
- Roasted Beet & Goat Cheese Bowl
- Asian Sesame Tempeh Bowl
- BBQ Jackfruit & Slaw Bowl
- Turmeric Roasted Cauliflower Bowl
- Warm Barley & Brussels Sprout Bowl
- Japanese Miso Salmon Bowl
- Fresh Berry & Yogurt Bowl
- Wild Rice & Roasted Carrot Bowl
- Tex-Mex Black Bean & Corn Bowl
- Moroccan-Spiced Quinoa Bowl
- Avocado & Soba Noodle Bowl
- Red Lentil & Curry Bowl
- Chickpea & Tahini Power Bowl
- Korean Bibimbap-Inspired Bowl
- Zesty Lemon & Herb Couscous Bowl
- Sweet Potato & Black Bean Bowl
- Roasted Squash & Pomegranate Bowl
- Spicy Kimchi & Brown Rice Bowl
- Thai Mango & Coconut Rice Bowl

- Pesto Zucchini Noodle Bowl
- Pineapple & Teriyaki Tempeh Bowl
- Summer Berry & Chia Seed Bowl
- Hearty Lentil & Spinach Bowl
- Sesame Ginger Tofu Bowl
- Roasted Eggplant & Hummus Bowl
- Italian Caprese Grain Bowl
- Matcha Green Tea Smoothie Bowl
- Spicy Peanut Butter Noodle Bowl
- Grilled Portobello & Rice Bowl
- Cinnamon Apple & Oatmeal Bowl
- Coconut Curry Cauliflower Bowl
- Roasted Garlic & Lemon Quinoa Bowl
- Blueberry & Almond Chia Pudding Bowl

Ingredients:

- 1 cup (185g) cooked quinoa
- 1 zucchini, sliced
- 1 bell pepper, chopped
- ½ cup (75g) cherry tomatoes, halved
- ½ cup (100g) roasted chickpeas
- 1 tablespoon olive oil
- 1 teaspoon garlic powder
- Salt and pepper to taste

Instructions:

1. **Roast Vegetables:** Preheat oven to 400°F (200°C). Toss zucchini, bell pepper, and cherry tomatoes with olive oil, garlic powder, salt, and pepper. Roast for 20 minutes.
2. **Assemble Bowl:** Place quinoa in a bowl, top with roasted veggies and chickpeas.

Ingredients:

- 1 cup (185g) cooked quinoa or brown rice
- ½ cup (100g) cooked chickpeas
- ½ cup (75g) shredded carrots
- ½ cup (75g) cucumber slices
- ¼ cup (60g) hummus
- 1 tablespoon lemon juice

Instructions:

1. **Assemble Bowl:** Place grains in a bowl, add chickpeas, carrots, cucumber, and hummus.
2. **Drizzle with Lemon Juice:** Serve immediately.

Ingredients:

- 1 cup (185g) cooked quinoa
- ½ cup (100g) chickpeas
- ½ cup (75g) cherry tomatoes, halved
- ¼ cup (40g) kalamata olives, sliced
- ¼ cup (30g) crumbled feta cheese
- 1 tablespoon olive oil
- 1 teaspoon dried oregano

Instructions:

1. **Assemble Bowl:** Combine all ingredients in a bowl.
2. **Drizzle with Olive Oil:** Toss and serve.

Ingredients:

- 1 cup (185g) cooked farro or quinoa
- ½ cup (75g) steamed broccoli
- ½ avocado, sliced
- ½ cup (50g) baby spinach
- 2 tablespoons green goddess dressing

Instructions:

1. **Assemble Bowl:** Place grains in a bowl, add broccoli, avocado, and spinach.
2. **Drizzle with Dressing:** Serve fresh.

Ingredients:

- 1 cup (185g) cooked brown rice
- ½ cup (75g) shredded red cabbage
- ½ cup (75g) sliced bell peppers
- ½ cup (100g) cooked tofu or chicken
- 2 tablespoons peanut sauce
- 1 tablespoon chopped peanuts

Instructions:

1. **Assemble Bowl:** Layer rice, cabbage, bell peppers, and protein.
2. **Drizzle with Peanut Sauce:** Garnish with peanuts.

Ingredients:

- 1 cup (185g) cooked lentils
- ½ cup (100g) roasted sweet potatoes
- ½ cup (75g) baby spinach
- 2 tablespoons tahini dressing

Instructions:

1. **Assemble Bowl:** Place lentils, sweet potatoes, and spinach in a bowl.
2. **Drizzle with Tahini Dressing:** Serve warm.

Ingredients:

- 1 cup (185g) cooked brown rice
- ½ cup (100g) baked tofu
- ½ cup (75g) steamed bok choy
- 1 tablespoon miso dressing

Instructions:

1. **Assemble Bowl:** Combine rice, tofu, and bok choy.
2. **Drizzle with Miso Dressing:** Serve warm.

Ingredients:

- 1 cup (185g) cooked quinoa
- ½ cup (100g) roasted sweet potatoes
- ½ cup (50g) sautéed kale
- 2 tablespoons tahini dressing

Instructions:

1. **Assemble Bowl:** Layer quinoa, sweet potatoes, and kale.
2. **Drizzle with Tahini Dressing:** Serve warm.

Ingredients:

- 1 cup (185g) cooked brown rice
- ½ cup (100g) black beans
- ½ avocado, sliced
- ¼ cup (30g) salsa
- 1 tablespoon lime juice

Instructions:

1. **Assemble Bowl:** Layer rice, black beans, and avocado.
2. **Top with Salsa & Lime Juice:** Serve fresh.

Ingredients:

- 1 cup (150g) cauliflower rice
- ½ teaspoon turmeric
- ½ cup (75g) roasted chickpeas
- ½ cup (50g) sautéed spinach
- 1 tablespoon tahini dressing

Instructions:

1. **Sauté Cauliflower Rice:** Cook cauliflower rice with turmeric for 5 minutes.
2. **Assemble Bowl:** Layer cauliflower rice, chickpeas, and spinach.
3. **Drizzle with Tahini Dressing:** Serve warm.

Ingredients:

- 1 cup (185g) cooked farro
- ½ cup (100g) sautéed mushrooms
- ½ cup (50g) wilted kale
- ¼ cup (30g) toasted walnuts
- 1 tablespoon balsamic glaze

Instructions:

1. **Assemble Bowl:** Place farro, mushrooms, and kale in a bowl.
2. **Top with Walnuts:** Drizzle with balsamic glaze.

Ingredients:

- 1 cup (185g) cooked sushi rice or quinoa
- ½ cup (100g) cubed tofu
- ½ cup (75g) shelled edamame
- ½ cup (75g) diced cucumber
- ¼ cup (40g) shredded carrots
- 1 tablespoon soy sauce
- 1 teaspoon sesame seeds

Instructions:

1. **Assemble Bowl:** Layer rice, tofu, edamame, cucumber, and carrots.
2. **Drizzle with Soy Sauce:** Garnish with sesame seeds.

Ingredients:

- 1 cup (185g) cooked quinoa
- ½ cup (100g) roasted spiced chickpeas
- ½ cup (50g) sautéed spinach
- ¼ teaspoon cumin
- 1 tablespoon tahini dressing

Instructions:

1. **Assemble Bowl:** Combine quinoa, chickpeas, and spinach.
2. **Drizzle with Tahini Dressing:** Serve warm.

Ingredients:

- 1 cup (185g) cooked orzo
- ½ cup (100g) cherry tomatoes, halved
- ¼ cup (40g) kalamata olives, sliced
- ¼ cup (30g) crumbled feta cheese
- 1 tablespoon olive oil
- 1 teaspoon dried oregano

Instructions:

1. **Assemble Bowl:** Layer orzo, tomatoes, olives, and feta.
2. **Drizzle with Olive Oil:** Sprinkle with oregano.

Ingredients:

- 1 cup (185g) cooked brown rice
- ½ cup (75g) shredded red cabbage
- ½ cup (75g) sliced bell peppers
- ½ cup (75g) grated carrots
- ½ avocado, sliced
- 2 tablespoons tahini dressing

Instructions:

1. **Assemble Bowl:** Layer rice, cabbage, bell peppers, carrots, and avocado.
2. **Drizzle with Tahini Dressing:** Serve fresh.

Ingredients:

- 1 cup (185g) cooked quinoa
- ½ cup (100g) roasted beets, diced
- ¼ cup (30g) crumbled goat cheese
- ¼ cup (30g) toasted pecans
- 1 tablespoon balsamic glaze

Instructions:

1. **Assemble Bowl:** Place quinoa, beets, goat cheese, and pecans in a bowl.
2. **Drizzle with Balsamic Glaze:** Serve fresh.

Ingredients:

- 1 cup (185g) cooked brown rice
- ½ cup (100g) stir-fried tempeh
- ½ cup (75g) steamed broccoli
- 1 tablespoon sesame sauce
- 1 teaspoon sesame seeds

Instructions:

1. **Assemble Bowl:** Layer rice, tempeh, and broccoli.
2. **Drizzle with Sesame Sauce:** Garnish with sesame seeds.

Ingredients:

- 1 cup (185g) cooked quinoa
- ½ cup (100g) shredded BBQ jackfruit
- ½ cup (50g) coleslaw mix
- 1 tablespoon BBQ sauce

Instructions:

1. **Assemble Bowl:** Layer quinoa, jackfruit, and coleslaw.
2. **Drizzle with BBQ Sauce:** Serve fresh.

Ingredients:

- 1 cup (185g) cooked quinoa
- ½ cup (100g) turmeric-roasted cauliflower
- ½ cup (50g) baby spinach
- 1 tablespoon tahini dressing

Instructions:

1. **Roast Cauliflower:** Toss cauliflower with turmeric and roast at 400°F (200°C) for 20 minutes.
2. **Assemble Bowl:** Layer quinoa, cauliflower, and spinach.
3. **Drizzle with Tahini Dressing:** Serve warm.

Ingredients:

- 1 cup (185g) cooked barley
- ½ cup (100g) roasted Brussels sprouts, halved
- ¼ cup (30g) toasted almonds
- 1 tablespoon lemon vinaigrette

Instructions:

1. **Assemble Bowl:** Layer barley, Brussels sprouts, and almonds.
2. **Drizzle with Lemon Vinaigrette:** Serve warm.

Ingredients:

- 1 cup (185g) cooked sushi rice
- 1 salmon fillet (grilled or baked)
- 1 tablespoon miso paste
- 1 teaspoon soy sauce
- ½ cup (75g) steamed edamame
- ½ cup (75g) shredded cabbage
- 1 teaspoon sesame seeds

Instructions:

1. **Prepare Salmon:** Mix miso paste and soy sauce, brush over salmon, and bake at 375°F (190°C) for 12-15 minutes.
2. **Assemble Bowl:** Layer rice, salmon, edamame, and cabbage.
3. **Garnish with Sesame Seeds:** Serve warm.

Ingredients:

- 1 cup (240g) Greek yogurt
- ½ cup (75g) mixed fresh berries
- ¼ cup (30g) granola
- 1 tablespoon honey

Instructions:

1. **Assemble Bowl:** Spoon yogurt into a bowl, top with berries and granola.
2. **Drizzle with Honey:** Serve fresh.

Ingredients:

- 1 cup (185g) cooked wild rice
- ½ cup (100g) roasted carrots
- ¼ cup (30g) toasted pecans
- 1 tablespoon balsamic vinaigrette

Instructions:

1. **Roast Carrots:** Toss with olive oil and roast at 400°F (200°C) for 20 minutes.
2. **Assemble Bowl:** Layer wild rice, carrots, and pecans.
3. **Drizzle with Balsamic Vinaigrette:** Serve warm.

Ingredients:

- 1 cup (185g) cooked brown rice
- ½ cup (100g) black beans
- ½ cup (75g) roasted corn
- ¼ cup (30g) diced tomatoes
- 1 tablespoon lime juice

Instructions:

1. **Assemble Bowl:** Layer rice, black beans, corn, and tomatoes.
2. **Drizzle with Lime Juice:** Serve fresh.

Ingredients:

- 1 cup (185g) cooked quinoa
- ½ cup (100g) roasted chickpeas
- ½ cup (75g) sautéed spinach
- 1 teaspoon cumin
- 1 teaspoon cinnamon
- 1 tablespoon lemon dressing

Instructions:

1. **Season Chickpeas:** Toss with cumin and cinnamon, roast at 400°F (200°C) for 15 minutes.
2. **Assemble Bowl:** Layer quinoa, chickpeas, and spinach.
3. **Drizzle with Lemon Dressing:** Serve warm.

Ingredients:

- 1 cup (185g) cooked soba noodles
- ½ avocado, sliced
- ½ cup (75g) shredded carrots
- 1 tablespoon sesame dressing
- 1 teaspoon sesame seeds

Instructions:

1. **Assemble Bowl:** Layer soba noodles, avocado, and carrots.
2. **Drizzle with Sesame Dressing:** Garnish with sesame seeds.

Ingredients:

- 1 cup (185g) cooked red lentils
- ½ cup (100g) roasted cauliflower
- ½ cup (75g) steamed kale
- 1 teaspoon curry powder
- 1 tablespoon coconut yogurt

Instructions:

1. **Season Lentils:** Mix with curry powder.
2. **Assemble Bowl:** Layer lentils, cauliflower, and kale.
3. **Top with Coconut Yogurt:** Serve warm.

Ingredients:

- 1 cup (185g) cooked quinoa
- ½ cup (100g) roasted chickpeas
- ½ cup (50g) baby spinach
- 1 tablespoon tahini dressing

Instructions:

1. **Assemble Bowl:** Layer quinoa, chickpeas, and spinach.
2. **Drizzle with Tahini Dressing:** Serve fresh.

Ingredients:

- 1 cup (185g) cooked white rice
- ½ cup (100g) sautéed mushrooms
- ½ cup (75g) shredded carrots
- ½ cup (75g) sautéed spinach
- 1 fried egg
- 1 tablespoon gochujang (Korean chili paste)

Instructions:

1. **Assemble Bowl:** Layer rice, mushrooms, carrots, and spinach.
2. **Top with Fried Egg & Gochujang:** Serve warm.

Ingredients:

- 1 cup (185g) cooked couscous
- ½ cup (75g) cherry tomatoes, halved
- ¼ cup (40g) chopped parsley
- 1 tablespoon lemon juice
- 1 tablespoon olive oil

Instructions:

1. **Assemble Bowl:** Layer couscous, tomatoes, and parsley.
2. **Drizzle with Lemon Juice & Olive Oil:** Serve fresh.

Ingredients:

- 1 cup (185g) cooked quinoa
- ½ cup (100g) roasted sweet potatoes
- ½ cup (100g) black beans
- ¼ cup (30g) diced red onion
- 1 tablespoon lime juice

Instructions:

1. **Roast Sweet Potatoes:** Toss with olive oil, bake at 400°F (200°C) for 20 minutes.
2. **Assemble Bowl:** Layer quinoa, sweet potatoes, black beans, and onion.
3. **Drizzle with Lime Juice:** Serve warm.

Ingredients:

- 1 cup (185g) cooked farro
- ½ cup (100g) roasted butternut squash
- ¼ cup (50g) pomegranate seeds
- 1 tablespoon balsamic glaze

Instructions:

1. **Roast Squash:** Bake at 400°F (200°C) for 20 minutes.
2. **Assemble Bowl:** Layer farro, squash, and pomegranate seeds.
3. **Drizzle with Balsamic Glaze:** Serve warm.

Ingredients:

- 1 cup (185g) cooked brown rice
- ½ cup (75g) kimchi
- ½ cup (100g) sautéed mushrooms
- 1 fried egg
- 1 teaspoon sesame seeds

Instructions:

1. **Assemble Bowl:** Layer rice, kimchi, and mushrooms.
2. **Top with Fried Egg & Sesame Seeds:** Serve warm.

Ingredients:

- 1 cup (185g) cooked jasmine rice
- ½ cup (100g) diced mango
- ¼ cup (60ml) coconut milk
- 1 tablespoon toasted coconut flakes

Instructions:

1. **Assemble Bowl:** Layer rice and mango.
2. **Drizzle with Coconut Milk & Top with Coconut Flakes:** Serve fresh.

Ingredients:

- 1 cup (185g) cooked quinoa
- ½ cup (100g) chickpeas
- ½ cup (75g) sautéed kale
- 1 teaspoon minced garlic
- 1 tablespoon lemon dressing

Instructions:

1. **Sauté Chickpeas & Kale:** Cook with garlic for 3-5 minutes.
2. **Assemble Bowl:** Layer quinoa, chickpeas, and kale.
3. **Drizzle with Lemon Dressing:** Serve warm.

Ingredients:

- 1 banana, frozen
- ½ cup (120ml) almond milk
- 1 tablespoon almond butter
- ¼ cup (30g) granola
- 1 teaspoon chia seeds

Instructions:

1. **Blend Banana, Almond Milk, & Almond Butter:** Until smooth.
2. **Pour into Bowl & Top with Granola & Chia Seeds:** Serve fresh.

Ingredients:

- 2 cups (200g) spiralized zucchini
- ¼ cup (60g) pesto
- ½ cup (100g) cherry tomatoes, halved
- 1 tablespoon pine nuts

Instructions:

1. **Sauté Zucchini Noodles:** Lightly cook for 2-3 minutes.
2. **Toss with Pesto & Add Tomatoes:** Top with pine nuts.

Ingredients:

- 1 cup (185g) cooked brown rice
- ½ cup (100g) cubed tempeh
- ¼ cup (50g) pineapple chunks
- 1 tablespoon teriyaki sauce
- 1 teaspoon sesame seeds

Instructions:

1. **Sauté Tempeh in Teriyaki Sauce:** Cook for 5-7 minutes.
2. **Assemble Bowl:** Layer rice, tempeh, and pineapple.
3. **Sprinkle with Sesame Seeds:** Serve warm.

Ingredients:

- 1 cup (240g) Greek yogurt
- ½ cup (75g) mixed fresh berries
- 1 tablespoon chia seeds
- 1 tablespoon honey

Instructions:

1. **Assemble Bowl:** Layer yogurt and berries.
2. **Sprinkle with Chia Seeds & Drizzle with Honey:** Serve fresh.

Ingredients:

- 1 cup (185g) cooked lentils
- ½ cup (75g) sautéed spinach
- ¼ cup (30g) crumbled feta cheese
- 1 tablespoon balsamic dressing

Instructions:

1. **Assemble Bowl:** Layer lentils, spinach, and feta.
2. **Drizzle with Balsamic Dressing:** Serve warm.

Ingredients:

- 1 cup (185g) cooked jasmine rice
- ½ cup (100g) baked tofu
- ½ cup (75g) steamed broccoli
- 1 tablespoon sesame ginger sauce
- 1 teaspoon sesame seeds

Instructions:

1. **Assemble Bowl:** Layer rice, tofu, and broccoli.
2. **Drizzle with Sesame Ginger Sauce & Top with Sesame Seeds:** Serve warm.

Ingredients:

- 1 cup (185g) cooked quinoa
- ½ cup (100g) roasted eggplant, cubed
- ¼ cup (60g) hummus
- ½ cup (75g) cherry tomatoes, halved
- 1 tablespoon olive oil

Instructions:

1. **Roast Eggplant:** Toss with olive oil and roast at 400°F (200°C) for 20 minutes.
2. **Assemble Bowl:** Layer quinoa, roasted eggplant, tomatoes, and hummus.

Ingredients:

- 1 cup (185g) cooked farro
- ½ cup (75g) cherry tomatoes, halved
- ¼ cup (30g) mozzarella balls
- ¼ cup (40g) fresh basil leaves
- 1 tablespoon balsamic glaze

Instructions:

1. **Assemble Bowl:** Layer farro, tomatoes, mozzarella, and basil.
2. **Drizzle with Balsamic Glaze:** Serve fresh.

Ingredients:

- 1 banana, frozen
- ½ cup (120ml) almond milk
- 1 teaspoon matcha powder
- ¼ cup (30g) granola
- 1 teaspoon shredded coconut

Instructions:

1. **Blend Matcha, Banana, & Almond Milk:** Until smooth.
2. **Pour into Bowl & Top with Granola & Coconut:** Serve fresh.

Ingredients:

- 1 cup (185g) cooked rice noodles
- ½ cup (100g) shredded carrots
- ½ cup (75g) sliced bell peppers
- 1 tablespoon peanut butter
- 1 teaspoon sriracha

Instructions:

1. **Mix Sauce:** Blend peanut butter with sriracha.
2. **Assemble Bowl:** Toss noodles with sauce, then add carrots and bell peppers.

Ingredients:

- 1 cup (185g) cooked brown rice
- 1 grilled portobello mushroom, sliced
- ½ cup (75g) steamed spinach
- 1 tablespoon balsamic dressing

Instructions:

1. **Grill Portobello:** Brush with olive oil and grill for 5 minutes per side.
2. **Assemble Bowl:** Layer rice, mushrooms, and spinach.
3. **Drizzle with Balsamic Dressing:** Serve warm.

Ingredients:

- 1 cup (240ml) cooked oatmeal
- ½ cup (100g) diced apples
- 1 teaspoon cinnamon
- 1 tablespoon maple syrup
- 1 tablespoon chopped walnuts

Instructions:

1. **Assemble Bowl:** Layer oatmeal, apples, and cinnamon.
2. **Drizzle with Maple Syrup & Top with Walnuts:** Serve warm.

Ingredients:

- 1 cup (185g) cooked quinoa
- ½ cup (100g) roasted cauliflower
- ½ cup (75g) sautéed kale
- 1 tablespoon coconut curry sauce

Instructions:

1. **Roast Cauliflower:** Bake at 400°F (200°C) for 20 minutes.
2. **Assemble Bowl:** Layer quinoa, cauliflower, and kale.
3. **Drizzle with Coconut Curry Sauce:** Serve warm.

Ingredients:

- 1 cup (185g) cooked quinoa
- ½ cup (75g) steamed broccoli
- 1 teaspoon roasted garlic
- 1 tablespoon lemon juice
- 1 tablespoon olive oil

Instructions:

1. **Assemble Bowl:** Layer quinoa and broccoli.
2. **Mix Garlic, Lemon Juice & Olive Oil:** Drizzle over bowl.

Ingredients:

- ½ cup (120ml) almond milk
- 2 tablespoons chia seeds
- ½ cup (75g) fresh blueberries
- 1 tablespoon sliced almonds
- 1 teaspoon honey

Instructions:

1. **Prepare Chia Pudding:** Mix chia seeds with almond milk and let sit for 2 hours or overnight.
2. **Assemble Bowl:** Top pudding with blueberries, almonds, and honey.

www.ingramcontent.com/pod-product-compliance
Lightning Source LLC
LaVergne TN
LVHW081330060526
838201LV00055B/2557